# Seventy Year ITCH

Humorous Short Stories
About
Senior Dating

JOHN SOWER

Seventy Year ITCH

Copyright © 2024 by John Sower

All Rights Reserved

No part of this publication may be reproduced, distributed, or transmitted in any form or by any means, including photocopying, recording, or other electronic or mechanical methods, without the prior written permission of the publisher, except in the case of brief quotations embodied in critical reviews and certain other non-commercial uses permitted by copyright law.

# Preface & Dedication

At age 62, I became suddenly single as my wife of 30 years sought greener pastures. I was surprised and unprepared to be a bachelor. However, I recovered, and for the next 12 years, I enjoyed being a senior single.

I met interesting and exciting women and had several relationships. I learned a lot about life and women. Eventually, I met the right woman, and we've been happily married for six years.

This book is dedicated to the women who helped me through this transition: my family and friends, and my wife, who helped with editing.

# Table of Contents

Chapter 1: Seventy Year Itch ............................................. 1

Chapter 2: My First Spinning Class ................................. 7

Chapter 3: First Time Kayaking ..................................... 16

Chapter 4: Movie Premiere ............................................. 23

Chapter 5: Would I Like to Go Beagling? ..................... 29

Chapter 6: Dance Class Frustrations ............................ 38

Chapter 7: Hiking the Billy Goat Trail ......................... 46

Chapter 8: Wine Tour Diary ........................................... 55

Chapter 9: Rehearsal Dinner Toast ............................... 65

Chapter 10: Pre-Marital Health Exam .......................... 76

Chapter 11: Wedding Toast ............................................ 84

Chapter 12: Digging My Own Grave ............................. 92

About the Author .............................................................. 98

# Chapter 1: Seventy Year Itch

Do you remember the movie "Seven Year Itch"? Marilyn Monroe moved into the apartment next door to a guy, and the rest of the story is obvious. That's sort of what happened to me.

I was neither married nor committed at the time. I'd had a one-year starter marriage and a thirty-year second marriage, which produced two sons and lasted until my wife got bored and divorced me. I have no hard feelings. Her lifestyle mixed her with successful, wealthy people; I was outclassed. Little did I know she had freed me for a decade of an enjoyable senior social life.

I was 70 and learning about senior dating – with some initial success. My life was on "cruise control," and I was ready for a change. My business was doing well; my income had doubled, my sons were educated, married, and in promising careers, and my health was good.

The first thing I noticed was her spectacular smile. I mean spectacular. It filled the room. If it didn't, then her full figure made up the difference. She was a beautiful blonde – like a fantasy.

Over time, I witnessed that men melted when she smiled at them. Some would smile when they saw her and be drawn to her almost magnetically if she smiled at them. Their wives, conversely, looked away and frowned at their stupidly grinning husbands.

I took her to meet a potential restaurant client one evening. He ignored me, walked over to her, held her by both arms and told her she looked stunning. She smiled because she did.

Another time, my partner stayed with her in my kitchen while I drove off for ice. When I returned, he was sitting close and singing to her – yes, singing. Her snug-fitting sweater may have hypnotized him. He had completely lost it. I've teased him about it ever since – but not in the presence of his wife.

Marilyn's brilliant smile in the "Seven Year Itch" makes the point.

I was a quiet, nerdy, plain-looking, bespectacled finance guy—a man that women wouldn't look at twice—but it was time for something new.

It was time to step out of character and scratch my 70 Year Itch. If not her, then who? If not now, then when? If not this, then what? It was time.

Single seniors know their adult children are not interested in their dating. Mine were busy young professionals with careers and children, and my new single social life was a low priority. They don't have a place in their brains for information about their single parents' dating. They were in denial. They knew that I had been a good father and husband and that their mother had been the one to end the marriage, but they were never comfortable with my dating.

I met a beautiful redhead neighbor soon after I became single, and the relationship moved rapidly. I had met her by telling the realtor who wanted to list our house that she could have the listing if she introduced me to a spectacular woman "just like her." The "just like her" phrase caught her attention – and she promptly did so – and she got the listing.

I took her (the redhead, not the realtor) to a jazz club with one of my sons and his wife. Both women liked jazz, but my son was stiff and uncomfortable seeing me in a new relationship.

A year later, my other son and his wife joined me and a woman I had just started to date for dinner. Afterward, as we walked out, I was surprised to hear him innocently ask, "What are your intentions with my father?" I don't think that's really what he meant, but he was nervous, and that's what he said. If I had known the question was coming, I would have cued her to say, "I'm just with him for the sex," which sadly for me wasn't true.

We met through a dating service. I was amazed that such an attractive woman would appear – but there she was. I enthusiastically pursued her and ensured she knew about our next date whenever we went out. She was very sociable and friendly, with a good sense of humor, an incredible figure, and that beautiful smile.

I've summarized the relationship as wine, sex, and rock and roll. We drank Pino Grigio wine from Northern Italy, a light white wine. I put ice cubes in mine to keep it cold. I kept a list on my phone that rated the Pino Grigio wines we tasted. The list was long, and our favorite was Santa Margherita. We had a favorite restaurant near her apartment, where we sat at the bar, had dinner, and drank Pino Grigio.

She moved into my condo. We were both morning people and had regular 8:00 am Sunday morning dates, which were terrific. Sometimes, we had dates at other times when we traveled.

We went dancing. She had taken ballroom dance lessons, and I struggled but learned fast dance steps like the East Coast Six-Step. We were pretty good and even received a few compliments.

On Friday nights, our favorite place was a roadhouse bar with a country-western singer. There was a regular crowd of enthusiasts, although the dance floor was small. We sat at the bar and had spaghetti Bolognese with our Pino Grigio. She was always the best-looking woman in the bar, and we both knew she was getting stared at, and I was getting envious glances.

I was careful not to have more than one glass of wine, and I drove home slowly to avoid problems. We usually stayed to close the bar, and our favorite song was, appropriately, "Closing Time" by Leonard Cohen.

Our favorite group was The Fabulous Hubcaps, an oldies rock band that performed in the Mid-Atlantic area. We followed them to different locations where they performed. We went so often that we knew the band members – you could have called us senior rocker "groupies."

My sons were tolerant but not open and welcoming. They were young and in love and didn't understand my state of mind. I knew what I was doing, but I was having a good time and not hurting anyone – so why not? I loved them and their kids but was living my own life.

We went to Northern Michigan on vacation and visited my high school friends. Afterward, the story was the same. The women didn't like her, but the men did. She didn't care and said she knew women never liked her.

We visited Nantucket, and late one evening, after we had been in several bars, we spoke with a female bartender about our relationship. She commented, "She's carrying you," which meant she was more attractive than me. We all laughed, and I agreed.

Her appearance was deceiving as she was an

attentive mother to her four grown children and a loving grandmother to her grandsons. Also, she cared about people. Once, when the elderly woman in the condo next to mine had a health crisis and was gasping to breathe, she stepped forward, took her arm, and spoke with her, which calmed her down and helped her - while my less glamorous neighbors stood by helplessly and ineffectively.

We both had many good times in our relationship, which lasted for several carefree years. Later, we realized we were incompatible, the bloom fell off the rose, and the relationship ended peacefully.

There was much fun and affection, but it wasn't love.

I had other dating relationships, and then I met a woman six years ago, and we got married. We've been very happy ever since.

While I'm not recommending that my long-time married friends take time off for an "itch," I certainly enjoyed mine.

I have many pleasant memories.

# Chapter 2: My First Spinning Class

I knew I was in trouble.

The young man at her fitness club desk said there were cancellations due to the snowstorm, and there was room for us in the spinning class starting in 10 minutes. I'd been so relieved two minutes before when he said the spinning class was full.

I was trapped. We'd just completed an 8:00 am tennis game, and she had beaten me. I had excuses like pains in my 60-ish legs and forgetting my Ibuprofen – but getting beat by a woman in any sport under any circumstances was traumatic. Usually, I could beat her – but not today.

I suggested that I'd happily wait for her at the nearby Starbucks. I pictured myself reading the Sunday New York Times, drinking my favorite Indonesian coffee, and napping in one of their wonderful, overstuffed chairs. I'm unsure if she teased, cajoled, or shamed me, but somehow, there I was - no Starbucks and no NYT in Spinning class.

I was still in my sweaty tennis clothes. She was, too, except she ran to the locker room and reappeared a minute later in a dry, sleek, form-fitting leotard and tank top – and a happy smile on her face – like a cat that had just eaten a mouse. She was happy that she'd beaten me at tennis, gotten me into spinning class, and made it in time for the start – like a little girl with a present to open. She's a trim, 50ish redhead, and she looked terrific.

She is fit, athletic, and attractive – which cannot be said about me. She has a Ph.D., a ten-page academic bio, and a long think-tank research list – again, nada for me.

We only met a few months back – both of us had been on the wrong end of a marital dumping, resulting in difficult divorces.

She talked a lot about Spinning class – and went several times a week – and how it made her feel energized and invigorated. I hadn't been on a bicycle in years. Maybe the last time was as a student in Amsterdam, when, after a tour of the Heineken brewery and too much lingering over free beers in the lounge, we took a ride in the country, enjoying the scenic canals and windmills. Then we realized that the ride home, against the wind, was much harder than the ride out – with the wind.

I had never been on a stationary cycle. My view of the

exercise was to walk nine holes with a pull cart on a beautiful day at my golf club – and then rest in the Adirondack chairs on the front lawn, watching birds on Chesapeake Bay.

She'd been a good sport and joined me a half dozen times to play golf – and she's pretty good. I guess it wouldn't kill me to pitch up for her sport – spinning - at least once - except that on second thought, maybe it would.

The spinning room was about 12 by 20 feet – with 15 stationary cycles in five rows of three cycles per row. In the front, on a low stage, was another cycle facing us – for the instructor, a fit young man who was our spinning host for the next 45 minutes.

There were only three other people – all men. This was the class that was supposedly full until it snowed. What are these spinners, a bunch of snow wimps – who can sit and spin a stationary cycle for hours but can't shovel and drive through a few inches of snow? We came over five miles from downtown to her suburban club.

I told the instructor that I wanted a bike near the back – in case I couldn't last longer than a few minutes and had to sneak out. He adjusted my seat and handlebars, and I was out of excuses, so I mounted up. She got on a bike beside me in the back row – between me and the door. Did she think she might have to block me from running away?

The music started, and just like that, we were spinning. The first thing one notices is that it is very easy – there is no resistance like a real bike. I was initially encouraged and thought I might be OK. Three or four minutes went by. I stole glances at her on my right. She's nice to look at in her long red hair, spinning tights, and tank top. The music got louder, and the instructor told us to "pick up the pace." I noticed that the three guys immediately did so - and so did she. Now, I began to worry. Were they taking this seriously?

I checked out the three guys. A young 20-ish guy on the right had an athletic build with broad shoulders, big leg muscles, and a narrow waist. He had on a dark blue leotard (he probably has a masculine name for it) with a black stripe down the outside, a blue and black long-sleeved skin-tight shirt (Is there a spinning uniform or "wardrobe"?), and a color-coordinated, blue-black scarf thing on his head.

I couldn't see much about the guy four rows in front of me – except that he was in the center of the front row, wearing a yellow and black bicycle racing shirt with black biking shorts. He was pedaling about three times faster than I was and was extremely serious about it. He was in his 40s and maybe was a former athlete.


The one on my left was eclectic. He was in his late 30s and was more casually dressed. He looked like a junior college professor. Should I tell him she had taught at

Princeton, Columbia, and Stanford? I didn't notice anyone else casually chatting and was mindful that I had to conserve energy.

The instructor repeatedly said, "OK, only a half minute left (on whatever tune he was playing at full volume), step it up." They all immediately reached the dial on the bike frame and turned it a half turn clockwise to the right to increase the resistance. Like the others, I reached down and, a casual observer might think, turned the dial. My hand did a half turn, but I let my fingers slip, so the dial turned no more than 1/4 inch. I did give it a real turn once and immediately could feel the increased resistance in my leg muscles, so I backed it off quickly. I still had 30 minutes to go and figured I couldn't make it for even 3 minutes at that level.

I used to have pleasant thoughts about "spin" or "spinning." As a child, it involved a favorite circus-colored toy top with a stem in the middle that I pumped to make it spin. When I had my first car in grad school, it was fun to take a spin, which meant driving my convertible in the country around Ann Arbor.

As a young married man, spinning meant surfcasting at sunset on Nantucket with an eleven-foot fishing rod and a large Penn spinning reel – and now and then hooking and battling a mighty bluefish. The word "spinning" would never mean the same after today.

The music was loud, but the only song I recognized was Soul Man – but I couldn't identify the artist. Was it

James Brown? I tried to get my spinning in sync with the beat of the music. I like to dance fast and think I have a good sense of rhythm – but I couldn't spin to the beat and am not sure why – I think I was spinning too fast.

I checked my watch, and only 15 minutes had passed – and I'd been spinning continuously. I straightened my back a few times, and the instructor had us stretch our arms and shoulders,

Once the instructor came back to check me out – perhaps to see if I was still alive – maybe he was worried whether his liability insurance payments were current. I complained about the bicycle seat – particularly the narrow front part. I'm not the most hung guy in the world – but where do you put them? I couldn't get comfortable. I tried shifting from side to side, and then when she wasn't looking, I tried reaching in and shifting them from side to side – but got no relief. If I'm leaning forward, spinning the stationary bike with the bike seat built like that – what does one do?

I told him truthfully that I'd read that these bike seats weren't healthy and could damage guys. She laughed, but how could she know anything about it? I looked at the other guys, and they didn't seem bothered. The instructor suggested padding – which seemed ridiculous to me because there wasn't enough room for them now – so what good would padding be?

I was getting tired, but we were only halfway through, so I played mind games to pass the time. My first is to pick a date a certain number of decades past, and then really, really focus on what I could remember about that time. Interestingly, by focusing hard for a while, the mind can recall an extraordinary amount. I used this trick to get me through a 30-minute MRI exam that was prescribed recently due to headaches from too much Starbucks coffee. I went back 50 years exactly – age 12 – 7th grade – February 1955 - in Ceylon (now Sri Lanka) with my family. I could write a book on what I remember that way – it's fun. I tried it again, returning only 40 years – age 22 – February 1965 - my senior year in college. Try it sometime!

Now, I was tired – but I'd made it past the halfway point without falling dead or wimping out – maybe I could make it all the way. I tried another mind trick I learned during my former wife's baby class: controlled breathing. By focusing totally on the in and out of one's breathing, one can divert the mind from pain – whether from an 8 lb baby being born or a dentist's drill – the technique is the same – and it works fine– for a while.

So now was the home stretch – clearly, we were around second base and sprinting to third. Could I keep it up? Would she be impressed if I could make it through the whole class? Would she like me more?

So, I rounded third, running on vapors. I had a mental picture of making it – but then falling outside the fitness club – like astronauts returning from outer space and trying to walk. Could I time it right so she would catch and hold me up?

I was desperate. How could I continue? In despair, I reached into my game bag of mental tricks and pulled out my trump card – the "mind out of body" technique. This is hard to do, and the science is questionable, but the technique focuses on imagining your mind leaving your body and positioning itself a few feet away watching. Like the breathing game, it puts the mind in some other place – where the body can't reach it to complain of pain.

So, we kept spinning and spinning and spinning and spinning and spinning and spinning and spinning and spinning. She had told me I didn't need to do what the instructor said, and the others did – like standing up and pumping – so I just sat and spun – with my mind just outside my shoulder, watching.

Finally, he said, "Only one more tune." – I could have shouted with happiness, so I used my absolute last mind trick – counting down from 100. This always works because it is tangible evidence that one is progressing, and the end is near. I got down to zero, only to learn he had lied – we were starting another tune after the "last" tune. Not fair! I'm dying here! Get me off this thing! So, I counted down from 100 again. He repeated it, saying, "I promise – this is the last." I could wring his skinny neck. Then it was over – but nobody stopped – so he played another tune. I was like one of the living dead.

Finally, when it was really over, the music stopped, and everyone stopped spinning; he correctly insisted that we stretch our legs. I could barely stand up but did so by holding onto the bike's handlebars. His last comment was, "Let's give a hand to the new guy – he made it." They all applauded me. That gave me enough strength to walk out the door without falling.

I had made it – my first spinning class. I hope I get invited again sometime.

She took my arm with a big smile as we walked out. Maybe I'll get lucky tonight.

# Chapter 3: First Time Kayaking

*"If your kayak tips over, and you are floating upside down in the water, you can turn right side up with an expert twist of the wrists and strong pull on the paddle."*

This is all I knew about kayaking – which I had learned by watching an expert kayaker on an airplane video several years ago as he turned over and over, in and out of the water, in his kayak.

With this image in mind, I was very nervous when she said she liked kayaking and suggested we go. However, I liked her; she was a good sport, and she was taking golf lessons to play my favorite sport with me – so I figured I was trapped and had to try – despite my fears of floating upside down beneath a kayak. My son says that in sailing, it's called 'turtling' because the only thing showing is the upside-down bottom of the boat – like a turtle shell.

That's not an image I want to experience.

She's a trim brunette, very pretty when she smiles or is embarrassed, and was my latest companion in my two-year experience with senior dating in my sixties.

I've been canoeing many times – even on the Potomac River – but not for 40 years. I'd never been kayaking before, but I finally agreed to go on a sunny, chilly October day. I hoped my indoor winter and summer golf exercise would sustain me, and I wouldn't embarrass myself by getting tired. We pulled into a marina on the Potomac River - South of Washington DC's Reagan National Airport. It was a public marina, and phrases like functional but not elegant come to mind when describing it.

I first noticed people paddling downriver in their rented kayaks as they left the marina. I thought to myself: Wouldn't it be smarter to initially paddle upriver – so that the current would be with you, not against you, when it came time to turn around and head back?

I remembered getting 'over-served' at the Heineken brewery in Amsterdam while in college, then renting bikes and having a wondrous time effortlessly riding along canals past windmills in the Dutch countryside – until we had to turn and head back – and only then realizing that in our 'altered' state, we hadn't noticed the favorable tail wind – until we had to peddle against it. The ride back was exhausting and took forever.

Would I embarrass myself by kayaking downriver but not having enough strength to paddle against the current and make it back? What would my alternatives be? Tie the kayaks together and have her pull me home? Call the marina for help and be humiliated when they came to rescue me in a power boat? Perhaps I could abandon the kayak along the riverbank and walk home – but wasn't it too marshy?

I was silently aghast when she ignored my suggestion for a two-person kayak and asked the marina attendant for two singles instead. What did she know that I didn't know? Why wouldn't she get in a kayak with me? Was she afraid I would tip us over?

The next thing I knew, a young man was sliding me backward down a carpeted incline, and I was floating in my kayak – alone. It was about 9 feet long, very narrow, and very tipsy. I had a 7-foot paddle with a 'blade' on each end.

She took off ahead of me through a channel of anchored sailboats heading for open water. She didn't seem very concerned about whether I was following her, stuck on the dock, or floating upside down with my head in the muck at the bottom of the river.

Her confident rhythmic stroke propelled her kayak rapidly with apparently little effort. I tried to copy her, but it wasn't that easy. The kayak tipped sideways with each stroke, so I had to brace my feet against the foot rail and counterbalance to stay upright. After each stroke, water ran down the paddle onto my arms and lap, which was disconcerting. I later realized that the rubber rings on my paddle, which were supposed to stop the water, were defective.

I gradually got the hang of it and looked for her. By then, she was several hundred yards ahead of me and was drifting towards a large white egret wading near a small island. She watched him through my binoculars. I was afraid to have them in the kayak because I feared losing them when/if I capsized. She was absorbed and had seemingly forgotten about me.

I've thought that birdwatching might be fun someday – especially if my golf game continues deteriorating. She seems to enjoy it, and it might be particularly fun if we took digital photos of the birds and then saved them in a digital scrapbook. I bought her a digital camera with a 10x telephoto lens for Christmas and look forward to future birding trips.

The egret flew away, and remembering me, she turned around and looked. I was catching up but got a little panicky when the kayaks drew alongside. I could see her giving mine a friendly little poke with her paddle and tipping me sideways into the water. I decided it was safer, although less romantic, to keep my distance.

She took off around the island and headed down river along the River's Western shore – so I followed her. We saw other birds: Seagulls, ducks, Canadian geese – plus a few more white egrets. I think we saw a great blue heron gliding low above the water. We were just South of the DC Beltway's Woodrow Wilson Bridge, where construction workers named two bald eagles George and Martha (after the former residents of nearby Mt Vernon), and we searched but didn't see any. One large dark and white bird may have been an osprey.

The riverbank is government property – and like any rivers that flood periodically, was strewn with both natural and man-made debris. Tree limbs, logs, and complete trees were scattered along the water's edge. There was also an abundance of rotted piers, flotsam from boats, and even some rusted steel scaffolding - perhaps from the foundations of the proposed Three Sisters Bridge that was wiped away in the 1972 Hurricane Agnes flood.

It was a beautiful, pleasant, peaceful sunny day, and we cruised quietly in the kayak along the river's edge. I tried to keep our downriver pace at a crawl, so I'd have enough strength to return to the marina. She'd done this before—presumably with other men—and I wondered if they were stronger than me and not worried about being embarrassed by collapsing from fatigue en route home.

We rented the kayaks for only four hours. I worried that, as in Amsterdam, the return would take twice as long, so after an hour and a half, I suggested we head home. She resisted, so we stayed longer, just floating and paddling leisurely along the riverbank. We floated close to flocks of ducks swimming along, which would scatter slowly as we approached.

The wind picked up – and it was from the Northeast – exactly the direction we had to go to get back around a large island. The sky darkened, and my fears heightened – we'd not only be paddling the river – but also upwind in a rain or windstorm – this might be a social disaster. It was at least a mile back to the marina. She didn't seem concerned, but she'd done it before. Also, she works out every morning – but I don't.

I suggested a race – thinking we could jump on the hardest part of the return route – before the winds picked up more. She took off immediately – I was amazed at how fast she moved–and her paddling strokes were smooth and rhythmic. She was ahead of me, but I didn't try to catch up – I just wanted to get us headed back before any gale-force winds hit.

I finally began to attain more of a rhythmic paddling stroke and was pleased with the speed I could maintain. I gradually caught up with her, or perhaps she let me, just as we turned the corner of the island and headed directly upriver toward the marina.

I saw a small power boat from the marina headed out to the middle of the river and thought – I guess they're going to rescue someone else – thank goodness it wasn't me.

Soon, I could see the marina and was relieved to realize I'd have enough strength to make it back. We stopped and coasted for a while, just enjoying the breeze, the pleasure of floating on the water on a beautiful day, and, perhaps, being together.

The exiting of a kayak is less than graceful. The attendant pulls the front of the kayak up on the carpeted inclined deck, and then you must try to get on your feet – from a sitting position facing uphill – with your bottom lower than your feet. It was very awkward and difficult.

As I struggled, she walked over, grabbed my arm, and pulled – which was a bit humiliating but was appreciated.

I didn't tip over, I didn't get wet, I survived my fears about kayaking, and I'd shared a beautiful day on the water with an attractive woman who I liked – and who, after seeing that I didn't tip my kayak over or embarrass myself – seemed to like me. We returned to the car and headed to a restaurant for a celebration and late lunch.

We have a compatible relationship, and I enjoy her company. We may go kayaking again in the spring, and next time, I will be less worried about 'turtling.'

# Chapter 4: Movie Premiere

She invited me to a movie premiere. That was exciting. I'd never been to a movie premiere before. She was exciting, too. She was tall, thin, beautiful, smart, witty, and full-figured. I had great hopes. She had a Ph.D. and had worked in President Reagan's White House. Now, she works for a conservative policy think tank.

We had only had three dates. The first was dinner in Georgetown (in Washington, DC), and the second was dinner and a movie. The third date was a reception honoring her 50th birthday that her friends hosted at a local restaurant.

After our second date, after we had finished a nice bottle of wine, we were walking in Georgetown past a store that sold sex aids and toys – or so I was told because I never visited it. As we walked by, she blurted out: "I've been married and divorced twice but never had an organism – so I bought a vibrator." I'm usually quick with a quip, but I was stunned and speechless. I thought about volunteering to help solve her problem but was too shocked to make a witty comment.

The movie premiere was at the Regal Theater on 7$^{th}$ Street in downtown DC. I suggested dinner at Bistro D'Oc on 10th Street, a country French restaurant.

D'Oc stands for Languedoc, a region in southern France along the Mediterranean coast west of the Province that is famous for bargain-priced wine and the 13th-century Albigensian Crusade, when the Catholics invaded and defeated the local Cathars, whom they believed were heretics.

The restaurant was near the downtown theatres and featured pre-theatre specials that could be prepared and served quickly. I arrived early, parked near the Theatre, and walked four blocks back to the restaurant along E Street to the restaurant. She arrived by taxi directly from work.

We had a nice country French dinner, but only 15 minutes before the movie started, we realized our bottle of Pouilly Fuisse wine was still half full. Perhaps unwisely, we started gulping it down. We left the restaurant with the bottle empty and only 10 minutes until showtime.

There's nothing worse than leaving good wine in the bottle. Pouilly Fuisse is a smooth French white wine made from chardonnay grapes from the Burgandy region of France along the Rhone River.

We then started our four-block walk to the Theatre. We got to 7th and E Streets – but couldn't find the Theatre (it is two blocks north of E Street on 7th and G Streets, and the entrance is set back from the street).

She panicked and suggested the premiere must be at the E Street Cinema – on E Street but four blocks back to 11th Street – near the restaurant where we had just had dinner. So, we hurried back four blocks, thinking we still had 10 minutes – and might make it.

Just before getting there – we realized that the movie was not at the E Street Cinema – like duh – I had carefully checked the address on the movie announcement – but the wine was kicking in and had erased my memory of where the theatre was.

So then, with three minutes to go – we knew we were in trouble. By this time, she had hoofed it across town twice in heels between 7th and 10th Streets, so we stopped on the sidewalk; she braced herself with a hand on my shoulder, opened her bag, and quickly changed from heels to tennis shoes. I wondered if she always carried tennis shoes on dates. Do women do that now? Was she thinking she might need to run away from me?

We then fast-walked five blocks from the E Street Cinema at 10th and E to the Regal Cinema at 7th and G.

She lived in the apartment building next to mine in

Georgetown but wouldn't visit my condo because she had rented a condo there the previous year and had been very ill from mold under the flooring (which was later remedied).

Her refusal to visit my condo and/or invite me to her next-door apartment didn't contribute to the romantic progress of our relationship.

We reached the theatre, but the drama wasn't over. We found the entrance and went up an escalator where two ticket takers said we were late and couldn't go to the Theatre. I thought for a second about punching one of them out, but there were two of them, and they didn't seem very threatened by me.

However, they took one look at her, in her tennis shoes, hair dis-shelved from running five blocks, her ample chest heaving from the exertion - and they hesitated.

She had that look in her eye that women get sometimes; you've all seen it, which suggested, "I hope you've enjoyed your life thus far because if you don't let us in NOW, you're going to be dead very soon." They let us in.

The drama wasn't over. The movie premiere was sold out, and it appeared there were no seats. I let her have the one seat we could find – and I went to the back row to beg some overweight, grumpy women to move so we could have two seats together.

I had used that line once before in a crowded restaurant in Rehoboth Beach. I asked my beautiful, blond date to wait at the door while I found seats at the bar. I found one seat and secured another by buying drinks to persuade a woman to move over. I then yelled to a guy near the door to "tell that blond there's a seat up here." He did, and she promptly joined me. Later, the guy told me, "I couldn't believe that line worked."

Anyway, don't you women hate it when you go to the theatre, get your big box of popcorn, get your extra-large coke, take your coat off, take your shoes off, put your bags and shoes under your seat – the movie starts, and you're feeling very comfortable - and then you are asked to stand up because some guy wants to get past you?

Then he disturbs everyone by talking to somebody else and begging them to move over one so he can have two seats together. He tells them a line about how he just got married and wants to sit beside his new wife.

Next, when you've gotten comfortable a second time, he comes back the other way, wanting out, and you must get up again, spilling your popcorn and maybe your coke, but you're saying thank goodness he's gone.

Then, of all things, he comes back in 30 seconds, just when you are getting back into the movie, and he wants to get past you again – so you must stand up again, spill your popcorn a third time – and this time stand there while some disheveled woman in tennis shoes goes past you as well.

When the movie ended, we waited until those women had left before we exited behind them. I was worried about getting whacked on the head with a large purse.

The movie was fun, and the evening was worth it. I forget the name of the movie that premiered, but it was anti-climatic compared to the excitement of our evening together.

The relationship didn't continue. I was disappointed, but one needs to expect and accept rejection in senior dating. Maybe, if I were head of a hedge fund, a high-level Republican strategist, or a connected lobbyist, she would have found me more appealing.

I had been rejected before, so I took it in stride and moved on. It's just part of senior dating.

I had been rejected a year before by a beautiful, redheaded Ph.D. liberal, so it gave me some comfort to know that my rejections were bipartisan.

# Chapter 5: Would I Like to Go Beagling?

She asked me with a sincere and pretty smile, which attracted me. I've explained to my granddaughter that smiles can be a secret weapon in the repertoire of female charms. We were in our 60s, divorced, healthy, active, and cautiously exploring senior dating.

I did not know what she meant, so I responded, "Sure…It sounds fun". Whatever Beagling was. When my son was a teenager, we owned a female beagle who was food-manic, howling, uncontrollable, and a handful even on a good day – so I was worried about what I had agreed to.

The setting was near Rectortown, a quaint town in rural Northern Virginia surrounded by historical markers about Civil War battles. It was in the Mosby Heritage Area, named after Civil War Confederate

Cavalry Captain John Mosby, whose raids terrorized Union forces.

We arrived around noon at a small, wood-frame house, which had seen better days. Overgrown pastures and unattended fencerows surrounded it. Soon, other people arrived, and the yard was filled with late-model cars and well-dressed people who had ventured out into the country for an adventure. The sun was shining on a chilly fall day, and they were wearing corduroy pants, sensible country shoes, thick sweaters, and appropriate fall outdoor wear. The brown and bright orange fall foliage created a magical atmosphere.

They reminded me of those naïve Washingtonians who, in 1861, ventured out to have picnics and watch the First Battle of Bull Run, only to retreat in panic when the Confederates overran the Union forces.

Our hostess invited us into the house to share chardonnay and charcuterie. Did she think we had to be fueled up for a rigorous country excursion?

We had been dating for a few months and enjoyed each other's company. We played golf, went to movies, attended concerts, went for long walks along the Potomac River, and dined at local restaurants. Our Beagling excursion was new for both of us. She was excited and cheerful. I secretly hoped she would find it romantic and increase her interest in me.

Foxhunting ("riding to hounds") was the sport of the English landed gentry. Years ago, at the Broadway Hotel, an ancient inn in the historic Cotswolds in England, I saw an early morning group of hunters in their brilliant red jackets, with their horses and foxhounds in the courtyard preparing for their hunt. Years later, my equestrian-enthusiastic stepdaughter advised me that the fox hunting jackets are called "pinks" after a famous British tailor.

On that same trip to the Cotswolds, my mother, a tea-totaling, Mid-West professor's-wife, had relished the luxury of Drambuie with her country oatmeal at a Broadway Hotel breakfast before venturing out to hike (aka "ramble") across the verdant English countryside to the iconic 18th century Broadway Tower on top of a ridge.

My son and his fiancé had joined us for the day. They had just become engaged and were swooning in dreamy, romantic ecstasy. They were more interested in each other than the Beagling. Oh, young love…why is it wasted on the young?

We didn't know what to expect. What was Beagling anyway? Are there rules? Was Beagling just middle-class foxhunting? Was Beagling the pastime of retired or disabled fox hunters who could no longer ride wildly over the fields, jumping fences and streams?

A station wagon pulled into the driveway, and the excitement level rose. A woman opened the rear door, and eight small beagles jumped out and milled around nervously. They knew why they were there and were twitchy, nervous, and excited – like children on Christmas morning before being permitted to open presents. They were almost identical, as if the same artist had painted them. Perhaps they were from the same litter – brothers and sisters.

The over-dressed and mostly overweight crowd poured out of the house to greet the new arrivals, and the noise level rose as there was a twitter of excitement in the air. Something was about to happen. They were out in the country on a beautiful fall day and ready.

People finished their chardonnays, grabbed the last morsels on the charcuterie board, and waited patiently. Several seemed to know what would happen next.

The woman guided the beagles with quiet commands – which we couldn't hear. She led them down a lane into an overgrown pasture toward a fencerow. What is a fencerow, the agriculturally challenged may ask? The space, including the wood fence post and barbed wire, and, in this case, the thorned bushes and brambles along each side of the fence, historically separated the farm fields. Farmers didn't want their cattle to go into the wheat or cornfields to eat the grain, so they built fences. Over time, with a lack of maintenance, the thorn bushes grew up along both sides of the fence – creating an ideal haven for rabbits – the objective of Beagling.

The woman slowly walked alongside the hedgerows, giving quiet commands to the Beagles. The guests followed behind. Some were still sipping their chardonnay and finishing the charcuterie board treats.

The beagles slowly canvassed back and forth, sticking their heads into gaps in the bushes and sniffing the ground. They were quivering with excitement; their tails were either wagging or sticking straight up, and now and then, one of them would let out a small, sputtering yip, which would provoke an answering round of small, sputtering yips and half-howls from the others. The woman seemed to know which yips and half-howls were false alarms, and she controlled the dogs and kept them moving forward.

There were several false alarms, but suddenly, one dog released a huge howl. Beagles don't bark; they howl. He had the fresh scent of a rabbit! The other dogs joined instantly and, in a frenzy, stuck their faces further into the bushes, trying to pick up the scent themselves. The gallant little dogs ran frantically around the bushes or jumped up to look over them, but the bushes were too thick, and the thorns were too painful – so they held back and howled in frustration. It was a frenzy. It was bedlam. It was crazy.

The dogs' excitement was contagious, and the guests also got excited and picked their pace from a stroll to a more determined pace in their newly purchased and well-shined country shoes. The fencerow was a long, gradual uphill climb, and some started to lag, perhaps regretting the 3rd or 4th glass of chardonnay and those last bites of cheese. The sun rose, and the air warmed, so the heavy jackets on top of the thick sweaters became a burden.

Then it happened. All at once, THERE WAS A RABBIT. A genuine, living, breathing, and running rabbit. We all saw him at once. He was about 40 yards ahead of us – but on the other side of the fence row – and calmly loping across the field away from us.

This was high drama! The dogs went crazy—they were ballistic! They howled at total volume and frantically plunged into the bushes, trying to reach the rabbit. We could see blood on their faces from the thorns.

The people also perked up. We all started yelling and cheering with excitement. The fox (aka rabbit) had been sighted, and the chase was on. The kill was imminent. You could almost smell the blood.

Perhaps in their chardonnay-enhanced excitement, people delusionally fancied themselves riding hellaciously over the fields, jumping the fences and hedgerows, dodging the tree limbs – chasing the dogs to corner the prey. I think they've seen these images in picture books.

Actually, the crowd only moved forward a little – but their pulses were faster, and their blood was up for the hunt.

It was exciting. The dogs were milling around

frantically – there was no resemblance to the well-disciplined pointers who hold their pose waiting for their command.

We could see both the frantic dogs and the rabbit. What would happen? Would the dogs catch and dismember the poor rabbit right in front of us? Suddenly, this seemed discomforting. The sight of rabbit blood and gore might not mix well with stomachs full of chardonnay and charcuterie, and it might splatter onto those expensive new country clothes and shoes.

We noticed the rabbit wasn't running frantically from the howling dogs. He was leisurely loping across the field away from them—like he was going for a casual jog in the country. The dogs could no longer see him but knew he was there. The rabbit didn't seem worried or endangered at all. He knew he was safe. He soon disappeared across the field, the dogs quieted, and the guests slowed down, albeit with some heavy breathing from the uphill, alcohol-dulled climb.

Perhaps, like the rabbit that supposedly threatened President Jimmy Carter, the rabbit would turn and counterattack, perhaps with hundreds of allies, and our lives would be threatened?

A beautiful description of passing on is in Watership Down, a complex story of rabbit culture and mortality. The aging hero gets weary while walking down a country lane at sunset, lies down to rest, leaves his body under a bush, and proceeds on his way into the darkness.

The rabbit was totally safe; the dogs couldn't penetrate the thick hedgerow bushes. There would be no dismembering, and there would be no blood and gore on this day. The dogs might continue to search – but they would never find that rabbit.

After all this collective exertion, the hostess suggested returning to the farmhouse for lunch. There was no resistance, and people applauded. The visions of heroic foxhunting vanished, the bathrooms beckoned, and the sun got hotter. Lunch sounded wonderful.

The hostess brought large trays of sandwiches, fruit, and more chardonnay. The conversation was lively and spirited as everyone retraced the excitement of the morning's hunt. The dogs licked their thorn wounds, and the owner tried to clean and calm them.

After lunch, the woman announced she would take the dogs along hedgerows on the other side of the house. The truth is that everything after that was anti-climactic. My son and his fiancé drifted off to do whatever young, affianced couples do when alone on warm afternoons – hardly bothering to say goodbye to us.

It got cloudy, which chilled the air, and we, too, decided to forfeit the afternoon hedgerow walk and call it a day. The morning adventures reminded me of long-ago fishing trips with lots of preparation, anticipation, and excitement in the conquest, but no fish.

A friend once explained that foxhunting was a higher social class activity than Beagling but that Beagling was a higher class activity than Basseting. I have a mental picture of comical basset hounds lumbering through the fields chasing something, with ears and sagging bellies dragging in the mud, and the more casually dressed followers swilling beer and munching hot dogs rather than chardonnay and charcuterie, but I've never had this confirmed. Also, I don't know what the Basseting might be chasing – gophers? Chipmunks? Does anyone know if this is true?

After the Beagling adventure, we returned home, had dinner, and then, possibly due to the romance of the Beagling, she agreed, for the first time, to spend the night at my place.

# Chapter 6: Dance Class Frustrations

She had been a ballet dancer. You could tell by how she moved – she didn't walk, she flowed. You could tell by her legs – her curvy calves. You could tell by how easily she learned new dance steps – Dancing was in her blood.

She had years of ballet classes and performances. We went to Ballets at the Kennedy Center. My favorite was La Bayadere, especially the haunting "Entrance of the Shades." I also liked The Nutcracker; years ago, I was awed by young Baryshnikov's soaring leaps.

She was small and beautiful, and as she said, her figure was very "curvy." She was a fitness enthusiast and regularly attended rigorous dance-type exercise classes at her gym. She was very private and reserved.

She liked dancing, but she was frustrated by my lack

of skill. I'd taken dance lessons in a previous relationship, but my instincts were poor, and my progress was slow.

I realized that if I wanted her to be happy in a relationship with me, I needed to become a better dancer, so I signed up for more dance lessons.

Some people like dancing simply for the fun of the music and the movement. They go to dance clubs and dance with different people just for the pleasure of it. The phrase "Joy of Movement" sums it up. I'm not one of those people. Not even close.

While I think dancing is fun, to me, it is part of a romantic relationship with a woman I'm interested in, and in the best cases, dancing is part of an evening that includes dinner and wine.

Guys in high school in the Midwest in the 1950s thought they were too cool for fast dancing, but when I was in college during the Beatles era, fast dancing was fun. We were jumping around individually, with no coordination as a couple, like in ballroom dancing.

I didn't like going to dance class and dancing with strangers, and she wouldn't go with me to lessons because she already knew how to dance – so I bit the bullet and went by myself.

I tried hard. I did.

I went to dance classes in DC for a few months – and learned the basics of the East Coast Swing – or six-step. It's a simple six-count step – but it was difficult for me to learn: Left, left, right, right, back step – over and over. It's good for fast music with a beat.

I took a year of dance classes at Arthur Murray. I hated them. First, we would practice some specific maneuvers, like not running into walls or, more interestingly, how to pivot when waltzing. Then, we were supposed to come back for an open class to practice with strangers, which I never did.

Next were private lessons in an instructor's living room; I paid extra for his female assistant so I wouldn't have to dance with him. I learned some steps – but soon forgot them.

Next was the Spanish Ballroom at Glen Echo Park for waltz lessons. They waltzed us up and down the long dance floor. But I could never get comfortable waltzing even though the Viennese waltzing on YouTube is beautiful.

Next was a dance hall in Virginia, coincidentally near where I'd lived with my parents when I was three years old, for lessons in West Coast Swing. I was getting comfortable with the East Coast Swing, so I felt confident – how hard could it be? It's hard, very hard. Think about imaginary parallel bars and couples moving back and forth between turning, spinning, and looking cool. Imagine is as close as I could get.

Perhaps the worst experience for me was trying to learn the cha-cha. We practiced in lessons I took several times, and sometimes I could remember the steps – for a little while. Later, I learned to sit down when they were playing the cha-cha. However, a stranger once asked my girlfriend to cha-cha with him, maybe because she looked bored sitting with me. I didn't like it even though she probably was.

Once, on a business trip to Fort Worth, Texas, I stayed in the Stockyards District, a historic area where cattle herds were delivered. After dinner, I walked to a local dance hall (not Billy Bob's with the famous raging bull). I watched as very cool cowboys did the Texas Two-Step. They danced their dates in a counter-clockwise circle around the dance floor in a slow-slow-quick-quick, slow-slow-spin-spin step with lots of spinning and rotating. I was determined to learn the Texas Two-Step and had several lessons but never mastered it. I guess I just wasn't cool enough.

When at the airport in Dallas, one sees those cool senior cowboys who are thin and have levies with sharp creases, expensive boots, fancy Western shirts, and big cowboy hats. I've been told they count their wealth in "units." One unit = $100 million. Sadly, I don't have any units. I've also heard that some of them are fakes – or as they say in Texas: "All hat but no cattle."

With a previous senior dating girlfriend, we went to a roadhouse bar in Northern Virginia on Friday nights when they had a country western singer we liked. There was a regular crowd, and the dance floor was small, so one got bumped a lot. We often stayed until the end and played one of our favorite songs, Leonard Cohen's "Closing Time," while driving home.

We also went to a large country western bar near the Baltimore airport and tried to learn line dancing. It looked fun, and my girlfriend picked it up quickly, but it was difficult for me, and I could never do it right. I should have spent hours at home practicing – but I didn't.

One of the coolest and most romantic dances is the Tango. I've watched it on YouTube and had one lesson, but I would never try it.

My worst experience was when we joined a ballroom dancing club with two other couples. We would meet in a country club ballroom on Sunday afternoons once a month, wearing tuxedos and gowns. We'd have a nice luncheon, and then the band would play.

They alternated between waltzes, swing tunes, foxtrot music, and others. It was great for enthusiastic dancers, but not for me. My date was always nervous that I wasn't dancing correctly; she would try to steer us if she thought we were likely to collide with another couple, and she was just unhappy with my dancing. I found her nervousness to be disquieting.

The best dancers were a couple with a large rec room in their home, where they practiced their ballroom dancing maneuvers. They flowed like professionals around the dance floor. He had retired from Exxon with a big pension.

It was always mysterious to me how, at these Sunday afternoon dance parties, some couples would dance gracefully together, round and round the dance floor, but be complexly oblivious to the beat of the music.

I always tried to follow the beat when dancing, whether the waltz, swing dances or slower numbers. I could never understand how they could dance so smoothly while ignoring the music's beat.

I did learn some fundamentals of ballroom dancing: There must be a leader (man) and a follower (woman), and it's up to the man to lead and make the woman look good. I learned to maintain contact in the dance position and gently pull or press to cue the woman's movements. I also learned to cup rather than squeeze her hand, watch ahead to avoid bumping into other dancers, and wear dance shoes so I didn't crush her toes.

I danced with my partner's wife at his daughter's wedding reception. It was a fast dance, and she tried to go alone or lead me. I reminded her that it's the man's role to lead and the woman's role to follow, and she responded, "I always have a problem with that." Was that a reflection of their marriage?

One basic maneuver in the East Coast six-step swing is when the man raises his arm to the left or the right. On the first left step, the woman quickly turns, goes underneath in a four-step count, and then the back step is done together. The woman needs to move quickly. If done properly, the man can lead the woman in various routines – to the same six-step beat. The man can stay in a central position and let the woman rotate around him – or join her in moving.

Over time, I became comfortable with the East Coast Swing and the Foxtrot, which is nice for slower music. The steps are slow, slow, quick, quick. We danced a lot, and she actually complimented me a few times after rigorous six-step swing numbers.

Sometimes, even now, when I hear an oldie with a beat, I'll move my feet to the six beat left, left, right, right, back-step.

Our favorite group was The Fabulous Hubcaps, a group of senior rockers who were together for 50 years and, sadly, announced they were retiring in 2023. We became "Hubcap groupies" and showed up where they played in different locations.

Our favorite dance locale was the Carlyle Club in Alexandria, VA, an elegant nightclub where we had a nice dinner with wine, danced to the oldies, and watched the Hubcaps perform.

We were together in a relationship for five years. We had close friends and many good times. One day, out of the blue, she handed me my condo keys, said we were breaking up – and walked out.

I never knew why. I asked, but she didn't respond. That's an inexplicable part of the drama of senior dating.

I have moved on but miss the six-step swing dancing

with her.

Maybe I was kidding myself by thinking my dancing had improved.

# Chapter 7: Hiking the Billy Goat Trail

My younger brother Sam was visiting, and we needed exercise after a hearty Thanksgiving dinner. He was an avid hiker who had walked all the trails around Moab, Utah. He was a healthy and fit 68, and I was 75. I regularly walked nine holes at the golf course, but I realized that age was catching up, and I was slowing down. We decided to hike the Billy Goat Trail.

My future wife, Mary, at 65, is a beautiful woman. In her 20s, she was stunning. I have 50 pictures of her at many ages that rotate through the digital picture frame on my desk. We later were married, but at the time, I worried that she might lose interest because I was ten years older.

Once, at age 20, she walked into a large New York bank seeking a job. The receptionist rejected her, but a vice president saw her, chased her down the street, and offered her a job just because she was so attractive. The same thing happened in the US Capitol. A Congressman offered her a job after only a glance. She is a smart, hard worker and was more than eye candy. Her father and her son are Mensa.

The website says the Billy Goat Trail is "the most difficult trail in the Washington, DC area." It starts north of DC on the Maryland (East) side of the Potomac River at the C&O Canal National Park and goes south along the river. The northern part, which we hiked, is the most difficult.

The C&O Canal starts in Georgetown in Washington, DC, and runs 185 miles to Cumberland, MD. It opened in 1831 and operated for 100 years, carrying coal, lumber, and grain in mule-pulled barges. It was saved in 1954 when Supreme Court Justice William O. Douglas led an 8-day hike along the canal towpath and called for its preservation.

The four of us included Mary, my brother Sam, her 16-year-old granddaughter Sue and me. It was cold, and we had warm jackets, jeans, and sturdy hiking shoes. A sign at the start of the trail says, "This trail will ruin street shoes." I had a walking stick, which helped in the hard spots.

After leaving the parking lot, the first part of the hike is about 300 yards south along the canal towpath. It was a holiday weekend, and other people were on the trail even though it was cold. Next, we turned to the right toward the river on a dirt trail full of rocks and tree roots. We followed blue blazes on the trees that showed us the trail.

Soon, we were on a high rocky plateau, maybe ten stories above the river. The scenery was beautiful, although the cold wind was biting. Despite the inclement weather, we could see fishermen on the rocks and kayakers on the white water rapids of the Potomac Gorge and were reminded that the river is fast and dangerous. Sadly, each year, there are deaths from people who fall in and are dragged under by the current.

Across the river in Virginia, we could see the Great Falls Park, with ruins of the canals of the Potowmack Canal Company, founded by George Washington in 1785. He wanted to open trade from Maryland and Virginia to the Ohio River Valley. Slaves built those canals, which opened in 1802 and survived for 26 years. It closed in 1828 and was followed by the C&O Canal on the Maryland side of the river. It was one of the first corporations in the country.

I have done a lot of hiking. When I was young, my brother and I hiked near my parent's lake-side cottage in Northern Michigan, including a long hike with our family dog around our 3-mile-long pear-shaped lake.

At age 12, in Ceylon (now Sri Lanka), we started climbing the 7,359 ft Adams Peak at midnight to be at the peak at dawn. Coming down was harder than going up because my legs got tired and were quivering. Men in our family are not known for strong legs.

Years ago, my company had executive planning retreats in Tucson, AZ. These retreats included long hikes among the majestic tall Saguaro and smaller flowering cactus plants in the foothills of Mt Lemmon, followed by hot jacuzzies, cold drinks, and warm food.

We also recently climbed nearby Sugarloaf Mountain, which was rigorous and fun—as was the rest stop at the nearby Sugarloaf Winery.

We stayed on the high plateau and continued south for several hundred yards. The terrain was rocky, so we had to step carefully.

We saw a dramatic sign that read: "Difficult Trail Ahead." It continued: "Many hikers are injured yearly on this section of the Billy Goat Trail. The terrain includes sharp drops, required jumps across open spaces, walking along the edges of rocks, and climbing up a 50' traverse." We were all silent after reading this sign. We were intimidated.

After this warning, we paused and plunged ahead. The trail changed and became very difficult. The website says we must "scramble over and around large boulders." That was probably an understatement. It was very hard going.

My future wife Mary and her granddaughter Sue nimbly jumped from boulder to boulder, and at a spry 69, my brother could too – or some of them, anyway. I quickly realized that my boulder-jumping days were behind me, and for the most part, I had to climb up and down them or make my way between them. After 100 yards, my brother caught up with me with a worried look and urged me to turn around and go back. Maybe he was concerned about what he would do with an injured or dead 200 lb 75-year-old brother on this difficult trail. I had hiked the trail before and knew what was ahead – and I told him he could go back to the car, but I was going on. He had no choice but to stay with us.

Years before, with my sons (ages 8 and 11) on the trail along with our rambunctious and undisciplined beagle, which I mistakenly took with us, we suddenly saw, only 20 ft ahead, standing alone and undeterred – a billy goat! I was stunned and speechless. Who expects to see a billy goat on Billy Goat Trail? The billy goat didn't seem worried when the beagle lunged toward him, nearly pulling me off a boulder into a deep crevice. I managed to hang on to the howling dog and pull her past the goat, which quickly and adroitly disappeared. To this day, I can't believe that happened. No one I know has ever seen a billy goat on Billy Goat Trail.

The trail continued to get harder, requiring me to climb up and over huge boulders. Finally, it descended, and after sliding down a ten-foot slope on our bottoms, we were on the sandy bank of the Potomac River.

I worried because Mary and Sue seemed quick and

nimble on the big rocks, but I was the opposite – slow and plodding. I was afraid I wasn't convincing her that I was a youthful and vigorous 75-year-old. She had gotten very quiet. Was it fatigue, or was she considering abandoning me in favor of someone younger?

Next, we had to go up five stories, described as "a steep climb along a cliff face." People used a long diagonal crevice in the face of the cliff ("a diagonal crack in the canyon wall.") as a path to inch their way up or down. I had deliberately planned our hike so that we would be climbing up rather than climbing down. If descending, one looks over the cliff's edge out to the river and far beyond – which is unnerving. I have mild acrophobia (fear of heights) and am more comfortable climbing up the cliff, where one sees only the cliff wall in front – rather than climbing down.

Sue, the 16-year-old granddaughter, looked at the cliff face and panicked. She wailed that she couldn't do it and, in tears, said she wanted to turn around and begged us to go back. She was very anxious – which scared us. I was afraid of a complete teenage emotional breakdown. I considered returning but was afraid I couldn't make it over the big boulders again. I also thought about having my brother take her back, but that would leave Mary and me on the face of the cliff by ourselves – alone.

We rested and watched the people creeping up the diagonal crevice and got up on our nerves. Sue calmed down, and after waiting for a group of teenagers who ascended comfortably, we started to follow them. Sue went first on her hands and knees most of the time. She calmed down, cheered up, and did surprisingly well. Mary followed – always watchful of her granddaughter. We inched up the cliff face. I was careful only to look forward because turning around and looking out into the abyss of sky and water would be too scary. I was afraid it might make me dizzy. My brother followed behind me.

Sue encountered a large, 6-foot-high rock close to the top. A strong young man reached down, took Sue's hand, and pulled her up—and she scrambled out of sight. Next, he reached down for Mary's hand and pulled her up, too, and they both disappeared.

I was alone on the cliff, facing a large rock to climb over and afraid to look back. My legs were exhausted and quivering like on Adam's Peak in Sri Lanka, and my brother was lagging far behind. Maybe he was afraid he might have to catch me if I started sliding or falling down the path. There was a crowd behind him.

I panicked. I knew I was in trouble. I didn't know what to do. Why had the strong young man abandoned me? Why had we stupidly decided to hike the Billy Goat Trail anyway? What had I done at this place on the trail 20 years before? I thought briefly about turning around and going back down – but that was impossible because of the crowd on the trail behind us, my fear of looking down, and the fact that Mary and Sue were already on top of the cliff. What could I do?

For one of the few times in my life, I lost it. I broke down. I completely lost my self-control. My life passed before my eyes. I felt dizzy and weak-kneed and was afraid I would faint, like when I foolishly drove my Dad's farm tractor into a swamp while exploring and got stuck in the mud, like when I totaled his Volkswagen in Southern Illinois while visiting a girlfriend during a high school Christmas vacation; like the first time I got into a football game in high school and was so excited that I ran onto the field without my helmet; and like when on a comprehensive Economics exam to graduate from college when I was supposed to write for two hours about the reasons for the "diminution of skewness of income distribution in the 20th Century in the US" and didn't know what diminution meant—in all these instances, thought processes just stopped.

I was like Senator Mitch McConnell on live TV. I just froze. My last thought was a quick flash image of a Coast Guard Helicopter coming to carry me away like in the George Jones country-western song "He Stopped Loving Her Today.' And then, somehow, I was on the top with the three of them. To this day, I don't know what happened or how I did it. My brother said I squirmed around rather than over the big rock and climbed to the top of the cliff, but I don't remember. He followed me and did the same.

The rest of the hike was anti-climactic. Exhausted, we gradually descended to the towpath and returned to the car. We were near Angler's Inn, where, long ago, I took my first girlfriend when she visited Washington, DC. The second floor was private and elegant – where one might secretly take another man's wife.

We stopped to rest and read the Park Service brochure and learned there were old gold mines in the area; we were on Part A of the trail, which was the most challenging of three parts, and the rapids below prevented ships from going further upriver thus Georgetown grew as a port by transferring grain and tobacco from the canal barges to ships bound for Europe and ultimately into Washington DC, the Nation's Capital and center of the free world.

Fortunately, Mary didn't abandon me for someone younger; we've been married for six years.

However, that was my last hike on those large boulders on the Billy Goat Trail.

# Chapter 8: Wine Tour Diary

When I became single at age 62 and started dating, I started learning about wine, an integral part of my new relationships. Each one introduced me to a new wine.

Previously, I knew little about wine. We drank beer in college and mixed drinks like gin or vodka tonics during my 2-year first marriage and 30-year second marriage. I remember having lobsters with Tanqueray gin and tonic at a roadside picnic in Bar Harbor, ME, with my first wife and bluefish pate with vodka tonics at cocktail parties in Nantucket with my second.

My first experience with wine was in Paris during college. We drank inexpensive red wine and ate delicious cheese and French bread while waiting for visas to attend an international work camp in Nigeria. I avoided red wine for years, thinking it gave me headaches and hangovers.

My first tasting experience wasn't wine. It was at the Heineken Beer Brewery in Amsterdam while in college. We toured the brewery and enjoyed the free samples afterward – but stayed too long. Then, we had the bright idea of renting bicycles, riding out into the Dutch countryside, and enjoying the artistic scenery of the canals and windmills. It didn't occur to us that the bike riding was too easy until, 10 miles out, we turned around and realized, to our chagrin, that we had been enjoying a strong tailwind, which then became a headwind. The return trip was grueling as the Heineken high wore off and the headwind strengthened.

One of the first things I did when becoming single was to buy "Wine For Dummies" to learn about wine. Next, I joined the French Wine Society and attended wine-tasting classes. I was puzzled how others could smell fruits like lemons and apples in wine when I could not smell anything. I almost asked a dumb question: Do they scatter lemons (or apples) along the rows of vines? The answer, as every wine expert ("Oenophile") knows, is: No – the taste and aromas in wine are from the interaction of the wine roots with the soil; the (Terroir") produces those tastes and smells.

**Sauvignon Blanc and Chardonnay**

My first post-marriage relationship was with a tall, liberal redhead with a Ph.D. in Sociology and a senior position in educational research at a think-tank. She liked jazz and white wines like Sauvignon Blanc and Chardonnay and would buy a half dozen bottles chosen at random. Our favorites were Pouilly-Fume and Sancerre, named after regions along the Loire River in France and made from Sauvignon Blanc grapes. Later, at a wine-tasting class, I learned that Sauvignon Blanc wines from New Zealand taste like grapefruit.

I learned much about Sauvignon Blanc wine in this relationship and about liberals – an interesting and unique subset of American culture. We traveled and had a fun year until she dropped me when she learned I voted for George W. Bush for President. I never liked jazz nor her oaky Chardonnay from California.

Further downriver (West) along the Loire River is the Viognier grape region, which I learned about in a noisy bar out of Sauvignon Blanc. The bartender shouted a suggested alternative, but I couldn't hear him. Finally, he wrote "V – own – yeah" on a napkin, and I said OK. It tastes like Sauvignon Blanc but is more complex.

**Pino Grigio and Champagne**

My next relationship was with a busty blond who liked Pino Grigio and Champagne. Pino Grigio is a dry, light white wine from Northern Italy. We had dinners at our favorite bars – and enjoyed different types of Pino Grigio. I kept a list of at least 50 wines on my phone, and we graded them. Our favorite was Santa Marguerita. Usually, after a few sips, I added ice cubes to keep the wine chilled and to stretch it because I limited myself to one glass when having to drive home.

On Fridays, we often went out dancing at a roadside Italian restaurant with a country-western singer we liked. We'd sit at the bar, nurse our Pino Grigios, eat spaghetti Bolognese, and enjoy the music, dancing, and each other.

I never liked champagne but bought it for our weekend morning mimosas. Eggs Benedict, fresh fruit, hot coffee, and cold mimosas are my favorite breakfast. Years later, I had breakfast with my future wife, her daughter, and her son-in-law at a restaurant that advertised "bottomless mimosas." We tested their staying power and our own, and we noticed that the waiter was slower to bring our third mimosa than the first and second. Regretfully, I had violated my only-one-glass rule.

**Cabernet Sauvignon**

Next was a petite former ballet dancer who liked red wines. We experimented with cabernet sauvignon ("cab"), Merlot, and Pinot noir and enjoyed all of them. In French Wine Society class, I learned that the so-called left bank vineyards (West of the Garonne River in Bordeaux) had rocky soil and produced the best cabernet sauvignon. The instructor brought a plastic bag full of gravel to the class and explained that the wine tasted best when the wine plants were stressed with the gravelly soil – compared to the rich soil on the right bank, which was better for Merlot. Thomas Jefferson enjoyed red wines from Bordeaux and bought them when he was in France and after returning to Virginia. A few years ago, there was a scandal about fake bottles of old red wine with the initials (T J) on them.

We hosted blind wine-tasting parties where we would tape paper around the bottles and then pour different red wines for each guest to guess what they were. We prefer cabernet sauvignon wines, especially those from California. We visited Napa with a group that included a retired executive who was a wine expert studying to be a wine judge. He made the arrangements, and we visited various wineries ranging from the large Castello Di Amorosa, styled like a 14th-century Tuscan castle, to small wineries with only a roadside stand. There are over 500 wineries in the Napa Valley to choose from.

One of our favorites was Frank Family Winery, and later, I spent a year buying all the 2013 Frank Family Cabernet Sauvignon I could find. I also bought four wine coolers to store it. We have purchased several bottles of their Patriarch Wine, which is expensive but worth it for special occasions.

One evening at dinner, our wine-judge friend facetiously told my girlfriend (a funny word for 70ish seniors) that she should think carefully about being with someone who put ice cubes in his Pino Grigio. Months later, I got revenge by holding an ice cube in a spoon, as if to put it in my red wine, while looking away from him, talking, and watching him squirm uncomfortably. I never put ice in red wine.

During my French Wine Society lessons, we were invited to a wine-tasting party at the French Embassy, and the invitation listed several expensive Bordeaux wines that would be available. I eagerly attended, hoping to taste some of those wines I couldn't afford to buy. I probably should have anticipated, but they quickly ran out of fine wines, so still, I have never tasted any of those $1,000+/bottle Bordeaux wines that Thomas Jefferson liked.

Experienced wine enthusiasts learn to swallow only a little wine at wine tastings, but that isn't easy if the wine is good. The problems from swallowing at wine tastings during the day are obvious. Also, at least one person must remain sober to drive home.

**Burgundy**

Burgundy red wine is from the Pinot Noir grape and is known only as Pinot Noir in California and Washington. We enjoy good French burgundy wines and dream about a burgundy wine tour supplemented with golf and good food, but it will probably never happen.

We are more familiar with French White Burgundy wines. One of the best-known is Pouilly Fuisse, supposedly a favorite of Jackie Onassis. My favorite is Puligny Montrachet, which is elegantly smooth. Both are from small towns in central France. We have served Puligny Montrachet, and it disappears quickly. Both are from chardonnay grapes.

I often try to find a good French White Burgundy on a restaurant menu if I order fish or chicken. An alternative is Alberino wine from Spain, which is similar but more complex.

**Rhone Wine**

We also like Rhone Wine, made from several grapes in the Rhone Valley. The most famous is Chateauneuf du Pape (Castle of the Pope), the Pope's vineyard when the French installed a pope in Southern France in the 14th century.

**Chianti and Sangria**

When thinking about Chianti wine, one may imagine cheap wine in small bottles in straw baskets with candles from the 1960s. However, I've learned there is more to Chianti.

While visiting Rome and Florence in Tuscany, we made a side trip to a winery. Despite language problems, we learned that they produced Chianti Classico and that the best was Chianti Classico Reserva, aged an additional year. It is good, but not our favorite.

Years ago, I had a dramatic encounter with Sangria when I was invited to present at an international economic development conference in Spain. The hosts took everyone to a bull ranch for an outing the evening I arrived. The only other American was a Congressional staffer for the appropriations subcommittee of the loan program I had pioneered. He was a very large man with a prodigious capacity for alcohol consumption, and I was fearful because I wanted to befriend him but knew I couldn't keep up with his drinking.

Bulls were grazing in the pasture, and dozens of glasses of Sangria were on a large table. I took two glasses, handed one to him, took a sip of mine, looked at the bulls, and turned to comment on the conference – but his glass was already empty. I knew I was in trouble.

I paced my drinking and survived the evening, made my presentation early the next morning with a fierce Sangria headache and hangover, and caught my plane out of Dodge.

After returning home, we invited him to dinner with the president of a trade association I had organized and our lobbyist. The lobbyist took him for cocktails before dinner, had three drinks, and arrived snockered. The association president and I alternated having three drinks each with our guest while he had six – so we were at three drinks each, and he was at nine. I don't remember anything about the rest of the evening except that he took all the desserts off the tray and ate them. Most importantly, he was, thereafter, our friend and supporter. Is this the way things always get done in Washington?

**Wine Class**

We enjoyed classes at the Capitol Wine School in Washington. My favorites were Cabernet Sauvignon and

White Burgundy. When we arrived for the cab class, they had a semi-circle of ten glasses with red wines on the tables in front of each seat. There were cabs from California and Washington, Bordeaux, Australia, South Africa, and Chile. They were all good, and it was great fun to taste them. There were about 20 people in the class, and most of the younger people didn't worry about swallowing the wine after each tasting. The noise level in the room rose during the evening and was at a pandemonium level at the end of the class.

Perhaps the best class was White Burgundy, which featured Pouilly Fouse, Pouilly Montrachet, and several others. A substitute teacher taught the class. I wondered if he had exceeded his budget by bringing such expensive wines.

I took a class sponsored by WSET (Wine & Spirits Education Trust), the global wine accreditation organization. I passed Level 1 and received a certificate, but the questions, especially on wine pairing, were very difficult. The certificate is framed on my wall, next to my wife's L'Academie de Cuisine cooking certificate, but I'm not trying to advance to higher levels.

Wine tastings are always fun. We enjoy stopping at roadside wineries to sample the wine, even in Northern Michigan, where local wineries sometimes have nice wines.

**Conclusion**

My senior dating relationships took me on a global

wine tour. My senior dating days are over, and now we are traveling together.

# Chapter 9: Rehearsal Dinner Toast

Does everyone know how they met? I wasn't there, but the story is that they felt chemistry during a romantic walk on the beach in Nantucket.

However, I was there for the proposal. How many brothers get to do that? We all went to Key West, FL, for Christmas and to play golf. Robert brought Leslie, and he chose that weekend to pop the question.

I'm in the middle; Robert is my older brother, and Carter is the youngest. Carter and I went to the Christmas Eve church service, leaving Robert and Leslie to have their evening.

He waited until after dinner and proposed marriage at a romantic setting on the hotel's pier out on the water. He said later that his cell phone buzzed all evening with friends asking whether he'd proposed yet. They were planning to go to the late church service but, due to the excitement of the moment, decided to start calling family and friends instead – and the rest is history – and here we are tonight.

He sent the engagement ring to me to prevent Leslie from seeing the box when it was delivered and becoming suspicious. I was nervous that someone might have seen the engagement ring-sized box and break into my condo to steal it, so I wrapped it in one of my golf socks (a clean one) and put it in my laundry basket, thinking that it was the last place a thief might look. Fortunately, there were no break-ins that evening.

The weekend's excitement for me was that Robert (and Carter) were both so distracted at golf on Christmas day that I beat them – probably for the last time ever.

**Robert**

A man doesn't get many opportunities to brag about his older brother in front of his family and friends, so here goes:


Our parents thought he might be an engineer when, at age 8, he gave them a cost analysis and budget for a requested model train set. They knew he would become an engineer when, at age 12, he spent three days in his room with the drawings and parts for an assemble-it-yourself, briefcase-sized, remote-control car Christmas present, and emerged triumphal to run it on the streets of Georgetown for the rest of the holidays.

They thought he might become a manager when, at age 18, he organized the weekend races at the Nantucket Yacht Club – and survived any serious injuries from those large sailboats or, more importantly, from their large ego owners. They knew he would as they watched him get his MBA and obtain years of increasing responsibility in large corporations.

They thought he might be a woman's successful life partner as they met the tall, beautiful, blond girlfriends who preceded Leslie, but we all knew he would as we came to know and love Leslie and watched them grow together, fall in love, and become engaged.

I'm allowed to brag here – and I can say that Robert's a very special man. With engineering, managerial, social, and personal skills – he will go far (especially with Leslie at his side) – and importantly, he will stay close to family. Leslie: I'm biased, but you've got yourself a keeper. You can bet long-term on Robert.

*Luckiest guy at the wedding*

I'm the luckiest guy at this wedding because I'm getting a sister. Robert is getting a bride – that took a lot more than luck. Big Albert (Leslie's father) is getting another son, but he already has one. Little Albert is getting a brother – but he's preoccupied with a new baby. Carter's getting a sister, but he already has a terrific girlfriend.

I'm the luckiest guy in this wedding - I'm getting a sister – which I've never had before. I'm very proud of my two brothers – but sisters are special – especially this one. I've loved getting to know her these past few years and look forward to being her brother-in-law. Thank you, Albert, Linda (Leslie's mother), and Robert– for letting me share.

*Best Man*

I have two terrific brothers, and I'm proud of both. The second and tallest is Carter, who has already been introduced and works in Wall Street's canyons in New York City.

Carter will be the Best Man tomorrow, but I'm worried about him. The word "best" may have gone to his head. There are rumors that a tall young man has been strutting around Wall Street saying, "I am the best man," "I am the best man," "I am the best man," "I am the best," and "I am the man." Does anyone know if these rumors are true?

I'm worried that he hasn't researched his "best man" responsibilities– so I decided to pitch in. He loves it when I help him. I learned on the web that the phrase "Best Man" evolved from the time of our medieval German ancestors – like those clans conquered by the Romans in the first scene of the movie "Gladiator" with Russell Crowe. Did everybody see that movie?

Back then, if a marrying-age young man like Robert spotted a beautiful maiden like Leslie in another clan, he would round up his brothers and buddies, get their swords, sneak off in the night, crash the maiden's homestead, and carry her back to their cave to be quickly married by the local priest. Where's Father Tom?

So, what, you ask, has this got to do with the title "Best Man"? Well, do you know what it means? I'm sorry, Carter, but in those days, "Best Man" did not mean "smartest man," it did not mean "biggest man," it did not mean "nicest guy," or "coolest guy." It does not even mean "tallest man" - although, in your case, it could. It means "best fighter." Why is that important? Because in those days, the bride's father, big Albert, the bride's Uncle Edbert, the bride's brother, little Albert, and their buddies might come – swords in hand - searching for Leslie – and there could be a nasty fight – and Carter, the "Best Man" would have been chosen because he was the "best fighter."

So Carter: As Robert and Leslie step forward to take their vows tomorrow, keep a close eye on big Albert, Uncle Edbert, and their friends because if they charge through the back of the cave - excuse me, I mean church, to stop the wedding – it's your responsibility as "Best Man" to be the "best fighter," and along with the groomsmen – to hold them off until the wedding ceremony is completed by Father Tom and the marriage is blessed by God. After that, it's too late – she's legally hooked. Right, Father Tom?

Are you up to that responsibility? Those Albert guys

look big. Do they teach you much sword-fighting on Wall Street?

Now, in truth, if the two Alberts do get out of hand tomorrow, I think a beautiful bride with fire in her eyes will push aside Carter and the fighting groomsmen and say, "Daddy. I love this man; I need you to please sit down—now," and the two Alberts would quiet down immediately, sheath their swords, and be seated.

Big Albert is pre-programmed so that when he hears Leslie say "I need" something, he stops what he's doing and reaches for his wallet. Right, Albert?

But if they didn't sit down, there would be <u>real</u> trouble because they would have to deal with an angry Linda (Leslie's mother) – a scary thought. She's been working on this wedding for months to make it perfect – I wouldn't want to be the one to disrupt it.

I recently had a tiny glimpse of that fire in Leslie's eyes when I innocently demonstrated my ignorance about grits – but I'll get to that in a minute.

*Wedding Ceremony*

Do you ever wonder why the groom stands on the right side of the priest? (when looking from behind). Because priests are smart (right Father Tom?), and they know that if the bride's father's war party crashes the wedding ceremony and the groomsmen are wearing swords, he stands less chance of being sliced if he is out of range as they draw their swords and turn around.

So why does the groom wear his wedding ring on his left hand? No one can do that old hand-shake trick, as in the movie Godfather, where someone holds the groom's sword hand to put a ring on—and he can't draw his sword and fight.

And why does the bride wear her wedding ring on her left hand? There's an old story that it's because her left hand is closer to her heart – representing love. That's romantic, but it's so the groom can drag her away from the fight and not squeeze and hurt her ring finger when he holds her right hand in his non-sword-carrying left hand – while wielding his sword and fighting with his right. Did you all know that?

I'm very proud of Leslie for surviving her first Northern winter. That's no small accomplishment for a Southern girl. But I understand there might have been some problems, so I thought I'd try to help. I've given Robert and Leslie their wedding present, but I have some special additional gifts for Leslie.

First, does anyone watch the TV show "America's Funniest Videos"? Maybe I should ask if anyone will confess that they watched it. I do. I love the scenes where pet dogs attack the mail when it's pushed through the slot in the front door.

I'm told that a similar phenomenon occurs at a condo in Beacon Hill in Boston. When the mailman is first heard, there is a glimmer of excitement. Then, when the mail is pushed through the slot, a tall blonde rushes for the door to scoop it up. Why? Because she's away from home, she's away from her parents, she's away from the South, she's homesick, and she doesn't get enough mail. Whose fault is that? All of us! How many of us did not send Leslie a card or letter at least once a month last winter? Shame on us!

So – to solve this problem – I'm passing out postcards – one for everyone here. Please use one to send Leslie a card or letter once a month for the next year.

Please tell her that you love her, that her family loves her, and that her new husband loves her. This is your responsibility – please take it seriously.

Second, all you Northerners – do you remember the winters when you were young? Do you remember how hard it was to keep track of all your winter clothing? You had mittens, hats, scarves, coats, snow pants, earmuffs, socks, boots, etc. Do you remember all that stuff?

Well, for some Southern girls experiencing their first Northern winter – keeping track of all this new stuff can be a problem. Sometimes, one gets the boots and coat – but forgets the mittens. Or one gets the boots, coat, and mittens – but forgets the hat or scarf – and then gets cold. Or sometimes one doesn't want to wear that bulky coat because one won't look trim and terrific – but then one gets cold. Isn't that annoying?

Do you remember what your mother did to help you with this problem? Did she clip the mittens to your coat?

Do you remember?

Well, life is more complicated now in the big city of Boston – and more than just two mitten clips are needed, so to help Leslie, I had a special clip ensemble built where she can clip all of her winter accessories together – coat, pants, boots, mittens, scarf, hat, earmuffs. I hope this makes her winters easier.

Third – another problem is remembering one's house key. Sometimes, when ready to leave the condo, one may look terrific and even have all the winter clothing, plus a purse, notebook, cell phone, shopping list, shopping bag, mittens, gloves, hat, boots, yadda yadda – and forget the house key – and then have to wait outside in the cold until one's husband-to-be comes home. Isn't that just so frustrating and embarrassing? Don't you hate it when you do that?

In the suburbs, one can easily hide a house key under a rock or flowerpot – but it's more difficult in a Boston high-rise condo.

So, to solve the problem, I've bought a rock for Leslie – with a secret waterproof compartment to hide a key. She can put an extra house key in the rock and put the rock out in the alley – and be confident in knowing that if she forgets her key, she can use the one in the rock – and still get in – and not wait out in the cold. It is safe because very few people steal rocks today – even in Boston.

Fourth – This last present is for Leslie and all of you Northerners. I mentioned before that several months ago, I innocently and casually demonstrated my ignorance about an important icon of Southern culture – grits. The totality of my knowledge about grits is from the movie "My Cousin Vinnie." Has anyone seen it? Robert: Do you remember the grits scenes?

I have never known what grits are – and had never eaten nor even thought about them. But I provide financing for businesses, and, in a recent e-mail to Robert about the menu for an engagement brunch for them at my condo in Washington, DC, I got several deals I'd financed years ago confused in my aging mind – including one business that re-cycled chicken manure – and it is remotely possible that I might have accidentally, innocently, and incorrectly suggested something about what grits are made of or from. I meant to say fertilizer, not grits.

Well, Leslie's Southern sensibilities were offended. She kept her cool, but I received a sizzling e-mail in response that, while polite, factual, academic, encyclopedic, and thorough – was very in-my-face with an attitude – that explained how grits are made from corn and expressed at the end with the words "so there!" Not a rude Northern "up yours," but a polite but firm, feminine, and Southern "so there!" – With an exclamation mark!

I love that e-mail, and I have it framed on my wall. It is so special that I've printed out copies for all of the Northerners here tonight so you, too, can learn about grits and avoid offending any Southerners by making the same mistake as mine.

## *Hope for the Future*

We are in this room and this city together tonight to celebrate and support Robert and Leslie's marriage.

We should all feel proud of our roles in raising, loving, and nurturing Robert and Leslie.

We should all feel proud of ourselves for how Robert and Leslie have turned out.

We should all feel proud of Robert and Leslie for who they are.

The results speak for themselves – We did well. We have done good.

Tomorrow is "payday," and we're being paid very well.

I think that their future together is bright.

I hope you enjoy the evening and the weekend.

Thank you for coming to Robert and Leslie's Rehearsal Dinner.

Please stand for a toast to Robert and Leslie, their wedding tomorrow, and their life together then after.

# Chapter 10: Pre-Marital Health Exam

My friend Ike is a very successful semi-retired junk bond arbitrageur who is rumored to have been a particularly aggressive and tough trader in his day. His fiancé, Marilyn, is an attractive blond who worries about Ike's health. She has an overly active schedule with charities and arts organizations. They enjoy a very affluent lifestyle, have been together for several years, and, per the rumors, have a lustful relationship.

They live in a beautiful Park Avenue co-op apartment building in Manhattan and have the intelligence, good fortune, and affluence to live better than many of us. We've tried to get Ike to take up golf for years – with no success. He is big-boned, robust, and strong but needs more exercise.

In their 70s, they were about to be married and

decided they should each get a pre-marital health exam. Marylyn went first and got a clean bill of health. Ike went to the doctor for his physical exam. He had been feeling listless and complained of having no energy. Marilyn was totally in love with Ike (as he was with her), and she canceled one of her many charity meetings, accompanied him to the doctor's office, and waited in the lobby during the physical.

The appointment seemed to take a long time, and Marilyn worried.

Finally, the doctor and Ike came out together to the waiting room. The doctor had a grim look on his face, but Ike seemed unconcerned. The doctor talked briefly with them and then asked Marilyn if he could speak with her privately. Marilyn's heart dropped, her knees felt weak, and she said, "Oh No! Ike has a health problem…what could it be?"

The doctor asked Marilyn to sit down. He paused to collect his thoughts and then explained that Ike was OK, but there was an issue – and it was particularly important that Marilyn understood and cooperated.

"What is it?" Marilyn said. I love Ike very much and want him to be healthy. What is the problem? I'll do anything for him—tell me."

"He has a condition known as EMS," said the doctor. "It's not unusual, and we've seen it before with aggressive businessmen. I haven't explained it to Ike because I don't want him to feel guilty. It can be treated.

However, it is serious, and if it isn't treated, it could be extremely serious."

"EMS?" thought Marilyn. She was too shy to ask what it meant, but she thought it sounded like one of the corporate stocks she'd seen on the list when Ike had explained his extensive stock and bond portfolio to her.

Finally, she asked: "What can I do for him?

"There are three things," explained the doctor. The first is diet. He needs to eat organic, freshly prepared food. He needs to have fresh fruit, vegetables, and salads every day—several times a day. He can't have any food from cans or that has preservatives. He needs to stick faithfully to his diet."

"I'll hire a girl to help prepare food," Marilyn said promptly. She already had a woman who came in to prepare their dinners, and she thought she could find a young woman to help with the daily preparation of fruits and vegetables.

"What else can I do? I love Ike very much and will do anything to help him." Marilyn said. She still didn't know what EMS stood for, but she was relieved that there was something she could do to help Ike.

"The second issue is his living environment," said the doctor. "He has to live in nearly sterile, totally clean surroundings with no dust and pollen."

"I'll hire a girl to help clean," said Marilyn. She was known as a fastidious homemaker, and she knew that with another girl to help, she could keep their co-op extraordinarily clean. "I'm happy to do that for Ike. I love him very much and will do anything for him." She still didn't know what EMS meant.

"What's the third thing?" Marilyn said. "Whatever it is, I'm sure I can find a girl to help him." She was worried about juggling her busy social schedule with all this extra help for Ike's health condition, but she loved Ike, and he came first.

The doctor paused and said, "You may want to re-think that. You need to understand that EMS stands for 'Excessive Masculinity Syndrome,' which is, as it sounds, the problem of his having excessive... uh...masculinity – which needs to be relieved, or he loses his energy – or worse."

Marilyn didn't understand at first. She was busy with her charity and arts activities but understood the need to hire a girl to prepare Ike's food and another to clean the co-op. But what was the doctor saying? Why couldn't she hire another girl for the third problem? Then she got it. It hit her. She understood the problem – and flushed with embarrassment.

The doctor continued: "He needs more...uh...' relief' than most men – even at his age. He is very... uh... masculine. If he doesn't get frequent 'relief,' then he has an internal chemical imbalance that weakens him and isn't healthy. The... uh... pressure builds up inside him, and at his age, it needs to be relieved – or he could lose his energy or, worse yet, die. No medicine can treat this. The only cure is relief."

"What exactly are you saying?" said Marilyn, feeling uneasy.

"He needs…' relief' fairly frequently – more often than other men."

"How often?" said Marilyn warily.

"At least every day," said the doctor, "actually twice a day – morning and night."

"Twice a day? You must be kidding. How bad is it if he doesn't?" she asked.

He paused dramatically and responded, "It couldn't be more serious." He stared into her eyes in response – but didn't say anything more. She understood.

Marilyn sat silently, furrowing her brow. Finally, she got up and walked out to the waiting room, deep in thought.

Ike stood up when she came out and, noticing her facial expression, said anxiously: "Lovey (his pet name for her) – what is it? Is something wrong?"

She didn't respond until they were in the elevator to the lobby. More anxiously now, Ike put his arm around her and asked again: "Tell me – what is it?"

Finally, she turned to him, paused, and then said sadly. "I'm sorry, Ike – but I'm afraid you're going to die."

***

Well, thankfully, he didn't die, but a few months later, he was feeling listless again, and he went back to the doctor for another check-up. In perpetual exhaustion, Marilyn slept late and didn't go with him. She struggled to juggle her charity and arts meetings schedule with Ike's new health requirements.

This time, the doctor was very grim. "I'm sorry," he said, "I hate to tell you, but I must. Your situation is very grave. It's worse than that. Your condition has worsened. I'm sorry to tell you – but it's fatal. There is nothing else we can do."

Ike, trying to be stoic, asked, after a pause, "How much time do I have?"

"Only 24 hours," said the doctor.

Ike went home alone, sadly, hugged Marilyn, and then told her. They held each other again, weeping. Ike hugged her again and then thought for a minute, hugged her once more, and said: "Well, Lovey, if I've only got 24 hours to live, and I was wondering if you would consider...you know..."

"Yes, of course," said Marilyn tearfully. "I love you more than ever and will do anything for you." And she did.

They slept afterward, got up, and had a late lunch – Ike wolfed down a can of his favorite soup, figuring it didn't matter about the preservatives anymore. They walked up Park Avenue together, one of their favorite pastimes, returned to the co-op, and took another nap.

On waking up in the late afternoon, Ike was feeling better and moved close to the snoozing Marilyn. After a while, she woke up, and he asked: "Lovey, I've only got 15 hours left, and I was hopeful that we could...well, you know."

Marilyn paused momentarily and then, remembering Ike's condition, said, "Of course, Ike. I love you very much, and I will do anything for you." And she did – again.

This time, they slept through the whole evening. Ike finally woke up hungry, raided the refrigerator, and ate a whole plate of sliced salami and sausages that Marilyn had forbidden him to eat because of the preservatives. Marilyn drowsily ate a slice or two, but exhausted, she stayed in bed and worried if she could get up for a committee meeting the next morning. Ike wandered around the co-op for a while, looking at the city lights and thinking about his life.

Finally, after emptying the refrigerator of all the preserved foods he could find, he recovered himself, and around midnight, he went back to bed. He tossed and turned, cleared his throat, turned his bed light on to read – everything he could to wake his sleeping, Marilyn.

Finally, he woke her up and said: "I'm sorry to wake you, Lovey, but I've only got eight hours to live, and I was hoping for ..."

There was a long silence this time, but then she

remembered – and agreed again reluctantly – afterward, they both went into a deep sleep.

Ike woke early – around 6:00 am- and lay there thinking. Marilyn didn't move. Finally, he nudged her, hoping to wake her up, but there was no reaction. Then he bumped her a few times with his arm, but there was still no reaction.

Finally, he shook her awake and said: "I'm sorry, Lovey, but I've only got…"

In desperate exhaustion, Marilyn interrupted him: "Ike, Give me a break! You don't have to get up in the morning – but I do!"

***

Thankfully, the doctor's diagnosis proved again to be incorrect. They were soon married and had a long and loving relationship.

# Chapter 11: Wedding Toast

Several years ago, we introduced our good friend Deborah, a big-time New York home decorator, to our best friend and 25-year neighbor Don, a power company executive. Both were divorced, so we sat them together at a dinner party – but Deborah didn't pay any attention to Don. A year later, we tried again, and this time, she did pay attention, and soon, they were engaged.

I was honored to be invited to speak at their wedding. While I'd done hundreds of presentations at conferences about financing and a few toasts at birthday parties, I'd never spoken at a wedding and was surprised to be invited. Further, I didn't have to just read from the bible or read a poem like the other participants – they said I was permitted to say anything I wanted – or so I thought.

The preparation of my remarks for the wedding was

a moving target – or perhaps a shrinking violet. When Don first called, he suggested I speak for 5-10 minutes. I'd never spoken at a wedding before. Still, they were adults, and I had a reputation for toasts that hinted at risqué, so I researched material on sexy seniors from the Internet and prepared a presentation that I thought was hilarious. Don and I spoke on the phone a week later, and I heard a female voice in the background saying, "Tell him 3-5 minutes," so I shortened my remarks and thought they were even funnier.

Don had initially said that my remarks could be humorous – but after another week, he got cold feet (or new instructions) and told me, "No jokes." I had spent hours on my presentation but had no choice, so I threw it away. Unsure how to proceed, I finally telephoned Deborah to get the straight scoop, and she told me "2 minutes," and it had to be "serious."

The wedding was in December, in an ancient church in Nantucket, and there was no heat during a record cold spell. We all had on topcoats – except for Deborah, who was in a beautiful strapless bright red wedding gown – with reportedly no underwear (a rumor I cannot confirm). Maybe she shortened my speaking time because she knew she would be freezing in the cold while I spoke.

When I took my turn at the podium in the church, people laughed in anticipation of hearing something risqué, and I had to wait for them to quiet. Then I did a somber two-minute presentation that went well – even though Deborah was shivering and turning pale before me. My opening line was, "It was <u>not</u> love at first sight for Don and Deborah." I told of their initial ineffectual meeting, their second encounter forced by us, and their rapid courtship. I quoted Paul in Corinthians, "Love is patient, love is kind," and Robert Browning's, "Grow older with me, the best is yet to be," and sat down.

In my toast at the wedding dinner, I said I had decided to research Don and Deborah. I wanted to discover the depth of their love and the probability of their marital success before standing up to speak for them. I explained that I had entered "Love" into Yahoo and noted that the first item was the "Love Calculator." Have you ever heard of the "Yahoo Love Calculator?"

To use the Yahoo Love Calculator, one enters secret confidential information about two people (actually, only their first names), and the computer analyzes – and predicts the probability of success of their love relationship.

I entered the names "Don and Deborah," and the computer returned with a 93% probability of a successful love relationship. I thought that's not good enough – but in comparison with what?

So, I entered my wife's name and mine because, after 27 years of marriage, I was sure it would say 100%. But it said there was only a 32% probability of success. Don and Deborah's 93% started looking good. A few months later, my wife surprised me by saying she wanted a divorce. What did Yahoo know that I didn't know?

What was disconcerting, however, was that I made a mistake and accidentally entered my name with Don's. It predicted 62% success – nearly double the probability for my wife and me – I guess it was appropriate that we were in Massachusetts.

Then, curious, I entered my name with my friend Ike, who is very nice and whom I'd always liked a lot. The computer whirred and clunked, then the screen blinked a few times, and then it went blank—like it was overloaded with emotion and couldn't express itself. I'm glad Ike's wife, Marilyn, was out of the room when I told the group about that.

She heard about it later and hasn't let me get near him since.

\*\*\*

There was a lull, so I made a second toast at the wedding dinner.

"This is Don's and Deborah's wedding. I thought about how to help them. It occurred to me that theirs is a potential culture clash of momentous proportions—a guy from the Midwest marrying a big-time New York home decorator." Like when actor Jack Nicholson described the experience of having sex with Brittany Spears: "It would be a life-altering experience."

This is classic Mars vs. Venus, and I looked around to

see who had a similar experience—I saw no one. Who, then, was most qualified to help? Me! I'm a Midwesterner with 27 years of marriage to a decorator. I decided that I, amongst all their friends, was uniquely positioned to offer my friend Don some advice. This gets close and personal, so be warned!

I was watching David Letterman, a Midwesterner from Indiana, when the thunderbolt hit me. So, I called in and spent some time with his staff last week preparing tonight's "Top Ten List." Are you all familiar with it?

Here's the Category: Top Ten Recommendations for a Man from the Midwest Marrying a Woman Who Is Big-Time New York Home Decorator:

10. Decorating is a Venus-type art form you will never understand. You are from Mars and will never get it – Don't even try – Get used to it.

9. Opinions - Never have a decorating opinion. It will be politely requested and even listened to, but it will be wrong. It will be ignored, stored away, and probably later criticized or used against you.

8. Vocabulary - Don't try to learn any decorating vocabulary. You won't ever know what the words mean and won't impress anyone if you use them. The words won't sound right coming from you, and whatever you say will be wrong. You don't know what the word "chintz" means, what it is, or where it comes from, and the truth is, you don't care.

7. Your Space—Establish your physical space—perhaps in the basement, garage, outbuilding, or barn. Do not accept any decorating suggestions for your space—not even one—that would be merely a foot in the door and a big mistake, resulting in color-coordinated upholstery, curtains, new furniture, knickknacks on every surface, and perhaps some chintz—whatever that is.

6. Decorate your space - Decorate, defining the word loosely, your own space your way. If you keep it the way you'd like it - perhaps like your garage or basement for the past 25 years, it will be too upsetting for the Venus-types to even be in there – thus, you will blissfully have privacy and peace.

5. Your stuff - Keep your stuff in your own space. Don't try to put any of it in the other parts of the house – it will mysteriously, perhaps in the middle of the night, be gradually demoted and moved further and further back in the house – to the guest rooms, later the basement, later the garage, and eventually the dumpster.

4. Shopping—Don't do any joint antiquing or shopping. As with decorating, your opinion will be politely requested and listened to—but ignored. Your role, if you do go, is to enthusiastically affirm Venus's purchases, help pay, and certainly carry.

3. Other women - Never comment about or show interest in any other woman – particularly their physical features. Venus types are emotional, jealous, and easily

hurt - and have steel-trap memories like elephants. When asked trick questions like: "Which of three gorgeous, stacked female movie stars do you think is most attractive – and why?" – pretend you don't hear or don't answer – or mumble something about going to the bathroom or basement and then leave the room. A truthful answer will only lead to detailed follow-up questions, hurt feelings, and long silences.

2. Previous relationships - Re-confirm, often, that you've never actually loved any other woman before – including any of your previous wives - certainly not in the way you do now. Any previous relationships were when you were young and irresponsible, and they had no meaning. Also, don't admit you remember much about previous women or physical relationships with them – and never discuss them.

1. Pre-marital virginity – This one's hard – Slowly establish the concept of your pre-marital virginity – even though this may initially appear inconsistent with your memory and the existence of your children – it's a nice line that is subconsciously comforting to Venus and will grow in truth over time with repetition. They say some people can maintain contradictory concepts in their minds – you can, too. Establish a good story and stick to it – no matter what. Your Venus will be much happier. If she's happy, you'll be happy too – marital bliss."

I never followed up to see if he followed my recommendations, but it didn't matter because they were divorced a few years later.

Welcome to the world of senior dating.

# Chapter 12: Digging My Own Grave

The occasion was my friend Joe's 60th birthday party. Joe is a successful real estate developer, husband, father, friend, and golfer—a hard act to follow.

Joe and Connie had been dating or living together for a long time, but their relationship had stagnated. Also, Joe had been having business setbacks, and his daughter had marital problems – and he seemed depressed. My wife urged me to give a toast at his birthday party that would cheer him up – and I tried.

People enjoy humor about personal idiosyncrasies and inadequacies, but to avoid hurt feelings, I've learned that the only person one can ridicule safely is oneself.

I made up a toast for the 25 guests at Joe's birthday party, which I described as a letter from my wife to her friend Marilyn that had not been mailed and that I had found.

"I was so encouraged last week after we discussed getting our husbands to change. Your success with Ike gives me a lot of hope. I know married couples are supposed to accept each other "as is"—warts and all—but your success is inspiring.

Unfortunately, after speaking with you, I spoke with my husband – and now I'm as discouraged as ever – he'll never change. I'm in a plane 35,000 ft high coming back from California, where I've been organizing my uncle's affairs. I feel good because I've been able to help at least one man change for the better – at least a little bit.

What is it with men? My husband is not bad, but I think how much better he could be - and how much happier I would be - if there were just a few changes.

1. <u>Interior design</u> – Take interior design; I'm in the business - it was my hobby and passion before opening my shops. Now, I am traveling the world, dealing with beautiful art and accessories, and meeting interesting people who share my interests. Some husbands are interested in interior design.

Like Joe, for instance, Joe and Connie's houses are beautiful and perfect. Joe is knowledgeable, interested, conversant, and talented in interior design.

My husband, in comparison, doesn't have a clue – and could care less. He is aesthetically neutral – or maybe I should say aesthetically neutered. If left alone, he would happily live in a minimalist condo overlooking the water – with off-white walls and a couple of historical maps for decoration. That would be it. Period.

**Why can't my husband be more like Joe?**

2. <u>Clothing</u> – And then there is the issue of clothing. Have you ever seen my husband in a suit or sport coat that wasn't dark blue – or in a suit that wasn't pinstriped? Have you ever seen him in slacks that weren't blue or gray – or boringly khaki? Joe wears a variety of colors, textures, and fabrics. Even Ike had yellow slacks the other night – he looked very sporty.

**Why can't my husband be more like Joe?**

3. <u>Sox</u> – Worst of all is his black sox. I'm so sick of them. How anal can he be? Other men, again like Joe, wear socks with nice colors, textures, and patterns – or, in the summer – no socks – like Ike. My husband thinks he made a big style move recently because he's wearing his black socks with cordovan loafers instead of black loafers. How pathetic!

**Why can't my husband be more like Joe?**

4. <u>Antiques</u> – Have you ever seen my husband join us to go antiquing? Both Joe and Ike do – and they enjoy it. I've been embarrassed several times when a group of us go antiquing and have a wonderful time – and he stays home and watches the golf channel – or reads the paper – or sleeps.

**Why can't my husband be more like Joe?**

5. <u>Golf</u> – Take golf – as the famous comedian said – please. Both Joe and my husband are enthusiastic golfers. They can both bore any social setting with golf talk. There is one big difference. Joe is both enthusiastic and skillful. He won a tournament earlier this summer. My husband, on the other hand, is only enthusiastic. I heard him say his scores haven't changed in years. He talks the talk but doesn't walk the walk.

**Why can't my husband be more like Joe?**

6. <u>Gifts</u>—The worst time is Christmas. Each year, I go to Brooks Brothers (the only store he will even consider for clothes) and buy some slightly more venturesome clothes for him—the phrase "slightly venturesome" means something other than blue or khaki. Our boys love the game, and they watch with anticipation as he opens the presents, inspects the clothes, politely says "no thanks," and puts them back in the boxes to be returned.

**Why can't my husband be more like Joe?**

7. <u>Building</u> – Everyone knows we built a new building for my shop in Nantucket. I worked extremely hard on both the design and the construction. I've received tons of compliments. Joe even wrote me a letter about it, which was so lovely that it made me cry. My husband hasn't said anything yet – except that he's a finance guy, and he's waiting to see the cash flow.

**Why can't my husband be more like Joe?**

8. <u>Humor</u>—A few years ago, my husband got over-served at a wedding and stood up and told a slightly off-color story—and, unfortunately, got lots of laughs. Now, he thinks he's a comedian and gets up and tells long, complicated stories. We've created a "humor monster." Someone, please help us. Joe gives short, appropriate toasts without trying to be a stand-up comedian.

**Why can't my husband be more like Joe?**

9. <u>Sex</u> – Last, but certainly not least, is the issue of sex...

My husband, well he............................................................................

But on the other hand, Joe............................................................................

**Why can't my husband be more like Joe?**

Marilyn: I'm sorry to unload this on you. Now, at least, I feel better. See you soon."

One last time:

**Why can't my husband be more like Joe?"**

My toast was well received.

Toward the end, everyone joined me: **Why can't my husband be more like Joe?**

Also, they gave me a resounding round of applause when I finished.

Joe was smiling, and whether attributed to me or not, their relationship improved; they finally were married, and they've been living happily ever since.

However, the toast backfired because the self-inflicted negative comments about me seemed to sink in, as a few months later, my wife said she wanted a divorce.

Without knowing it, I was digging my own grave with my birthday toast.

That was my unplanned and unexpected start to 12 years of fun senior dating.

I finally found the right woman and have been happily married for over six years.

# About the Author

John Sower, a finance executive and author, lives with his wife outside Washington, DC. He has always enjoyed humor and says these stories have been in his mind for years, if not decades. All he needed to do was sit down with a computer, and the stories told themselves.

This is the third in a series of Humorous Short Stories:

- "Snow Golf" - Humorous Short Stories about Golf
- "Seventy-Year ITCH" - Humorous Short Stories about Senior Dating
- "No Helmet" - Humorous Short Stories about Embarrassing Moments in Sports

All are available on Amazon.

John Sower

www.ingramcontent.com/pod-product-compliance
Lightning Source LLC
Chambersburg PA
CBHW050303120526
44590CB00016B/2470